How to Read Calendars and Clocks

BY KATE CONLEY

The Child's World®
childsworld.com

Published by The Child's World®
1980 Lookout Drive • Mankato, MN 56003-1705
800-599-READ • www.childsworld.com

Photographs ©: Shutterstock Images, cover (foreground), cover (background), 3, 10, 13, 18, 23; Sergey Novikov/Shutterstock Images, 5; Weekend Images Inc./iStockphoto, 7; Mikhail Morosin/Shutterstock Images, 9; iStockphoto, 11; Nadya Kubik/Shutterstock Images, 15; Sean F. Boggs/iStockphoto, 17; Serr Novik/iStockphoto, 19

ISBN 9781503823358
LCCN 2017944994

Printed in the United States of America
PA02360

ABOUT THE AUTHOR

Kate Conley has been writing nonfiction books for children for nearly two decades. When she's not writing, Conley spends her time reading, sewing, and solving crossword puzzles. She lives in Minnesota with her husband and two children.

Table of Contents

CHAPTER 1

Tracking Time

Close your eyes. Imagine something that can fly without wings. It moves forward, but not backward. Once you lose it, you can never get it back. What could this amazing thing be? Time, of course!

People use calendars and clocks to measure time. Clocks keep track of hours, minutes, and seconds. Calendars divide a year into months, weeks, and days. People rely on these tools every day. Calendars and clocks help people make plans and stick to **schedules**.

What kinds of clocks do you use?

Calendars and clocks come in many styles. But they all do the same thing. They keep people on time and organized. These simple tools bring order to everyday life.

CHAPTER 2

Using a Calendar

People use calendars every day. Calendars are **charts**. They help people keep track of long periods of time. Each year has 365 days, 12 months, and 52 weeks.

All calendars have basic information. They list the month and year. Calendars often have **columns** and **rows**. The days of the week are usually labeled at the top along the columns from left to right. The days of the week usually start with Sunday and end with Saturday.

Each row in a calendar **represents** one week. There are about four weeks in one month. Each box in a calendar stands for one day.

The first day of the month is numbered 1. Each month has between 28 and 31 days. The days are often numbered from left to right and from top to bottom on a calendar.

Calendars can help you make plans.

Some calendars have other information, too. They might list **holidays**, such as New Year's Day or Halloween. Monthly calendars also might show the previous month and the next month in small print at the top or bottom of the page. These **features** can help people use their calendars to plan events and stay organized.

Written dates follow a special order. First, the month is written as a word. Then the day and year follow it as numbers. A comma separates the day and year. An example of this style is *January 27, 2020*.

MONTHLY CALENDAR

Current Month

Year

JANUARY 2018

SUNDAY	MONDAY	TUESDAY	WEDNESDAY	THURSDAY	FRIDAY	SATURDAY
31	1 New Year's Day	2	3	4	5	6
7	8	9	10	11	12	13
14	15 Martin Luther King Jr. Day	16	17	18	19	20
21	22	23	24	25	26	27
28	29	30	31	1	2	3

Days of the Week

Holiday

Date

DECEMBER 2017

S	M	T	W	T	F	S
					1	2
3	4	5	6	7	8	9
10	11	12	13	14	15	16
17	18	19	20	21	22	23
24	25	26	27	28	29	30
31						

FEBRUARY 2018

S	M	T	W	T	F	S
				1	2	3
4	5	6	7	8	9	10
11	12	13	14	15	16	17
18	19	20	21	22	23	24
25	26	27	28			

Previous Month

Next Month

Another way to write the date is using only numbers. The month is written first, according to its order in the year. For example, January is the first month of the year. It is often written as *01*. Next are the day and year. Each part of the date is separated by a slash. If you were to write the date *January 27, 2020* as a number, it would be *01/27/2020*. This is the way dates are written in the United States. Other countries may write dates using different systems.

Calendars on electronic devices are easy to carry and use.

In the past, all calendars were on paper. They usually hung on a wall in a home or an office. Today, people use electronic calendars, too. They are often on smartphones. This makes calendars easy to carry anywhere. Phone calendars can also send reminders so you do not forget an event.

CHAPTER 3

Reading Clocks

Think about the activities you did yesterday. How did you use your time? Did you need to wake up at 8:00 a.m. to catch the bus? Did you meet a friend at the park at noon? Each of these events requires a clock.

A clock is a machine that shows the time. One type of clock is called an analog clock. An analog clock usually has a face and three hands. The face has the numbers 1 through 12 around it. The hands are like arrows. They point to the numbers on the clock face.

ANALOG CLOCK

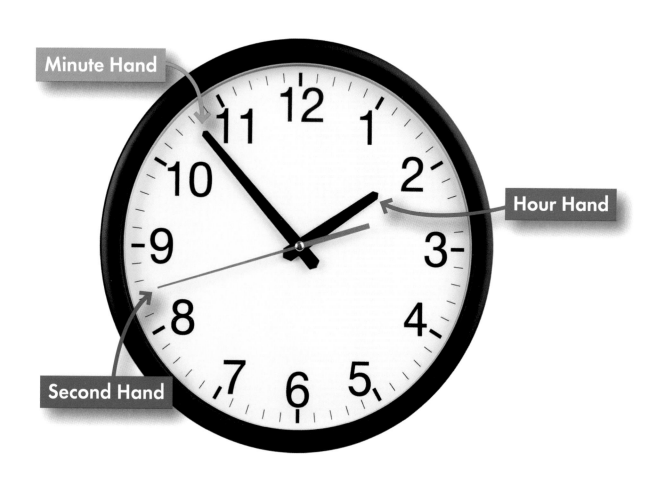

Minute Hand

Hour Hand

Second Hand

The short hand on an analog clock is called the hour hand. The number it points to stands for the hour. The long hand is called the minute hand. The number it points to stands for the number of minutes. Starting with the number 1, each number equals five minutes. When the minute hand points to the number 6, it means 30 minutes have passed. When the minute hand gets up to the number 12 again, that means 60 minutes have passed. Sixty minutes is equal to one hour. The minutes then start over again at 0.

Another hand on an analog clock is called the second hand. It is narrower than the other two hands. It is often red. The number it points to stands for the number of seconds. Starting with the number 1, each number equals five seconds.

Some kinds of wristwatches have small analog clocks.

When it reaches the number 12, 60 seconds have passed. Sixty seconds is equal to one minute. Then the seconds start over again at 0.

Digital clocks also show the time. But they do not have hands and a face. Instead, they have a display with digital numbers. The numbers change as time moves forward. Digital clocks have bright displays. This makes them easy to read even in the dark. Many alarm clocks are digital clocks.

People often need to share a specific time when making plans. Times can be written in two different ways. Sometimes people use words, such as *ten o'clock*. Other times they might use numerals, such as *10:00*. Both mean the same time.

When people give a time, they add the letters *a.m.* or *p.m.* The letters *a.m.* stand for "ante meridiem." This is Latin for "before midday." Times that take place in the morning use *a.m.* The letters *p.m.* stand for "post meridiem."

This is Latin for "after midday." Times that take place in the afternoon or at night use *p.m.* For example, "10:00 a.m." is in the morning, and "10:00 p.m." is at night.

Alarm clocks help people wake up and start their days.

Many kids learn how to tell time in school.

18

You can use clocks and calendars together to stay organized.

Knowing how to read calendars and clocks is a life skill. It can help you be on time. It can also help you make plans and stay organized. Now you know how to read all kinds of calendars and clocks!

1. How would you write out 05/01/2020?

    A. March 10, 2020

    B. May 1, 2020

    C. May 1, 2002

2. How many weeks are in one year?

 **3.** What does "a.m." stand for?

     A. post meridiem

     B. after midnight

     C. ante meridiem

 **4.** What is the purpose of a clock's short hand?

GLOSSARY

charts (CHARTZ) Charts are tables or diagrams that give information. Calendars are charts.

columns (KAHL-uhmz) Columns are lines of things that run up and down a page. On a calendar, the days of the week are usually labeled at the top along the columns.

digital (DIJ-uh-tuhl) Something that is digital has a display that shows numerical digits. Many alarm clocks are digital clocks.

features (FEE-churs) Features are important parts of something. Features of a calendar might include the previous month and the next month.

holidays (HAHL-uh-dayz) Holidays are special days for celebration. Many calendars list holidays.

represents (rep-ree-ZENTZ) Something that represents stands for something else. In a calendar, each row represents one week.

rows (ROHZ) Rows are lines of things that run left to right on a page. Many calendars have rows that run through the days of the week.

schedules (SKEJ-oolz) Schedules are written lists that show the order of events. Calendars and clocks help people stick to schedules.

TO LEARN MORE

In the Library

Cleary, Brian P. *A Second, a Minute, a Week with Days in It: A Book about Time.* Minneapolis, MN: Millbrook Press, 2013.

Loughran, Donna. *Time Ticks by: How Do You Read a Clock?* Chicago, IL: Norwood House Press, 2013.

Vogel, Julia. *Measuring Time: The Calendar.* Mankato, MN: The Child's World, 2013.

On the Web

Visit our Web site for links about how to read calendars and clocks:
childsworld.com/links

Note to Parents, Teachers, and Librarians: We routinely verify our Web links to make sure they are safe and active sites. So encourage your readers to check them out!

INDEX

ANSWER KEY

1. **How would you write out 05/01/2020?** B. May 1, 2020

2. **How many weeks are in one year?** There are 52 weeks in one year.

3. **What does "a.m." stand for?** C. ante meridiem

4. **What is the purpose of a clock's short hand?** The short hand on a clock tells you the hour.